Welcome to South Africa

By Patrick Ryan

The Child's World®

Welcome to the WORLD

Published by The Child's World®
1980 Lookout Drive
Mankato, MN 56003-1705
800-599-READ
www.childsworld.com

Content Adviser: Professor Gichana C. Manyara, Department of Geography,
Radford University, Radford, VA
Design and Production: The Creative Spark, San Juan Capistrano, CA
Editorial: Emily J. Dolbear, Brookline, MA
Photo Research: Deborah Goodsite, Califon, NJ

Cover and title page photo: Roger De La Harpe/Gallo Images
Interior photos: Alamy: 7 (Eric Nathan), 11 (Interfoto Pressebildagentur), 18 (Thomas Cockrem),
3 top, 22, 25 (Eric Nathan), 22–23 (Neil Cooper), 29 (David Pearson); AP Photo: 27 (Denis Farrell);
The Bridgeman Art Library: 10 (South African Library, Cape Town, South Africa); Getty Images: 15
(Alexander Joe/AFP), 19, 30 (Per-Anders Pettersson) 20 (Tom Stoddart); The Image Works: 21
(Jason Laure); iStockphoto.com: 28 (Ufuk Zivana); Lonely Planet Images: 14 (Craig Pershouse), 3
bottom,16 (Richard I'Anson); NASA Earth Observatory: 4 (Reto Stockli); Panos Pictures: 13 (Jon
Spaull); Peter Arnold, Inc.: 8 (Walter H. Hodge); PhotoLibrary Group: 24; SuperStock, Inc.: 6 (Steve
Vidler), 3 middle, 9 (age fotostock), 17.
Map: XNR Productions: 5

Library of Congress Cataloging-in-Publication Data
Ryan, Patrick, 1948–
 Welcome to South Africa / by Patrick Ryan.
  p. cm. — (Welcome to the world)
 Includes index.
 ISBN 978-1-59296-977-7 (library bound : alk. paper)
 1. South Africa—Juvenile literature. I. Title. II. Series.

DT1719.R93 2008
968—dc22

2007038145

Contents

Where Is South Africa?

Imagine that you could float high up in the air. If you looked down at the Earth, you would notice that the world has many land areas that are surrounded by water. These land areas are called **continents.** Many of these continents are made up of several different countries.

South Africa is a beautiful country on the continent of Africa. It has green grasslands, towering mountains, and hot deserts.

This picture gives us a flat look at Earth. South Africa is inside the red circle.

Did you **know?**

An entire nation lies inside South Africa. It's the tiny nation of Lesotho.

4

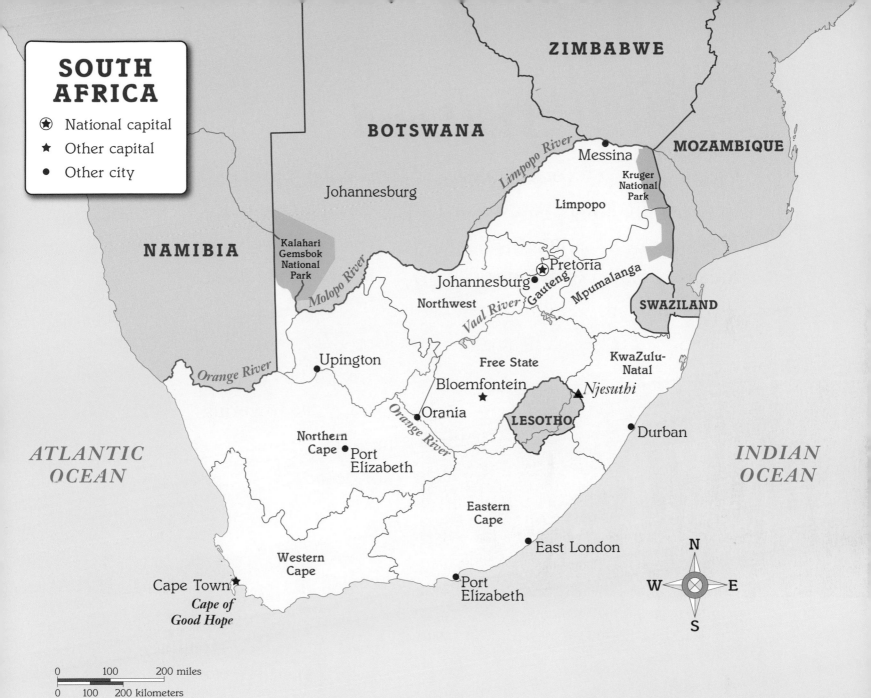

SOUTH AFRICA

- ⊛ National capital
- ★ Other capital
- ● Other city

ZIMBABWE

BOTSWANA

MOZAMBIQUE

Limpopo River

Messina ●

Johannesburg

Kruger National Park

NAMIBIA

Limpopo

Kalahari Gemsbok National Park

Molopo River

Pretoria ⊛

Johannesburg ●

Gauteng

Mpumalanga

SWAZILAND

Northwest

Vaal River

Orange River

Upington ●

Free State

KwaZulu-Natal

Bloemfontein ★

Njesuthi ▲

LESOTHO

Orania ●

Orange River

Durban ●

Northern Cape

● Port Elizabeth

ATLANTIC OCEAN

INDIAN OCEAN

Eastern Cape

East London ●

Western Cape

Cape Town ★

Port Elizabeth

N

W ⊗ E

S

Cape of Good Hope

| 0 | 100 | 200 miles |

| 0 | 100 | 200 kilometers |

The Land

The countryside of South Africa is made up of flat sections of land called **plateaus.** South Africa's plateau area is surrounded by mountains called the Great Escarpment. The highest mountain in South Africa is called Njesuthi (en-je-SU-tee).

The Great Escarpment stretches across several countries, including South Africa.

Part of the Orange River borders South Africa and Namibia.

South Africa sometimes doesn't get enough rain. Because of this, there are very few rivers. The three major rivers are the Orange, the Vaal, and the Limpopo. The Orange River is the longest. It is about 1,300 miles (2,092 kilometers) long!

Plants and Animals

Many rare animals live in South Africa. Elephants, lions, giraffes, zebras, and leopards all can be found there. Baboons,

A cycad plant growing in South Africa

crocodiles, and snakes live in South Africa, too. Each year, thousands of people visit the great national parks where the animals are protected. The largest and most famous national park in South Africa is Kruger National Park.

There are also many rare plants and grasses in South Africa. For example, the cycad is a huge tropical plant that has been on this planet for a very long time. It can sometimes grow to be more than 60 feet (18 meters) tall!

8

A herd of giraffes drinks at a water hole in Kruger National Park.

Long Ago

The first people in South Africa lived on the grasslands in small **ethnic groups.** Then, more than 300 years ago, people from Europe started arriving in South Africa. The first settlers were from Holland. At first, the Africans and their

This painting shows Dutch settlers landing in Cape Town in the 1600s.

A whites-only taxi sign in Pretoria in 1972

new neighbors got along. But slowly, they began to fight over the land. The Europeans and the African groups were soon at war.

In 1910, the Union of South Africa was formed. It was a government run only by white people. This government brought the country together, but it did not bring peace. Many people did not think it was fair that only white people could run the government.

Soon, the government set up a system called **apartheid** (uh-PAR-tite). Black people had to use separate buses, restaurants, and restrooms. White and black children couldn't even play together. Many South Africans wanted to end apartheid, but it took many years.

Did you **know?**

Apartheid means "apart" in the **Afrikaans** language.

11

South Africa Today

In 1994, **free elections** in South Africa were held for the first time. An African man named Nelson Mandela became the first black president of South Africa. He was a brave leader who spent more than 25 years in prison for fighting apartheid.

Mandela wanted the country to be governed by everyone, not just a few people. He left office in 1999. He played an important role ending apartheid and setting up a new, fair government. In today's South Africa, there is hope for peace, equality, and a better future.

Did you know?

Today, the disease called AIDS is a serious problem in South Africa. The country has the most AIDS patients in the world.

South Africans hold a poster of Nelson Mandela before voting in 1994.

Black South Africans make up most of the population.

The People

A South African boy carries his sister outside their home in Orania.

The years of apartheid were hard on black South Africans. While many white people were able to buy fancy houses and nice clothes, most black South Africans had to live in the poor areas and work at low-paying jobs. Today, this is changing. Without apartheid, black South Africans have more chances to educate their children, get better jobs, and earn more money.

More than three-quarters of South Africans are black. Most black South Africans are **Bantu.** About one-tenth of South Africans are white. The rest have mixed or Asian backgrounds.

Did you know?

South Africa has many different Bantu groups. They include the Zulu, Xhosa (KOH-sah), Pedi, Ndebele (ehn-dul-BEL-ay), Swazi, Tswana, Sotho (SU-too), Venda, and Tsonga people.

15

City Life and Country Life

South Africa's cities are very much like the cities in the rest of the world. Tall buildings and busy streets are common sights. Some cities have parks and fountains, too. City people live in apartments or houses. They drive cars or ride buses to get from place to place.

Almost half of black South Africans live in the

A shopping street in Johannesburg

Some people say Zulu huts look like beehives!
These huts are located in KwaZulu-Natal.

country. In the area called KwaZulu-Natal (kwa-ZOO-loo-na-TAL), the Zulu people farm and raise cattle. They live in huts that are made from reeds and straw. There aren't any windows in the huts and the floor is made of packed dirt.

Schools and Language

Schoolchildren in South Africa usually speak and read in more than one language. Many children in the lower grades study in the language of their ethnic group. Then in the upper grades, many students learn English. They also learn the Afrikaans language. With so many different languages, students in South Africa need to work hard. They also study history, math, and science.

Did you know?

The Zulu of South Africa use beads (right) to communicate. They even write each other "love letters" with different patterns of red, white, and green beads.

South African students use computers in their math class.

The country of South Africa has 11 official languages. They are Afrikaans, English, and nine Bantu languages. Zulu and Xhosa are the most common Bantu languages in South Africa.

19

This South African pours gold at a mine.

Work

For many years, South Africa was known as "the land of gold and diamonds." Many people worked in the country's mines to gather the sparkling stones.

Today, the people of South Africa have many other kinds of jobs. Factories in the cities produce machinery and clothes. South Africa also has many people who work in the fields. There they grow and harvest many things. South Africa's main crops are corn, wheat, sugar, potatoes, tobacco, and fruit, including grapes for wine.

A worker counts piles of rough stones at a South African diamond house.

Food

Foods from many different countries have found a home in South Africa. The Dutch, the Greeks, the Germans, the Chinese, and the Indians have all added some of their cooking traditions to South African dishes. For example, German sausages called *boerewors* (BOOR-uh-vors) are popular.

A favorite food in South Africa is **mealie pap.** Mealie pap is a thick porridge made with corn and milk. Many South Africans also like to eat ostrich eggs!

Sausages called *boerewors* cooking on a grill

South African students being served mealie pap

Local people and tourists enjoy a Cape Town beach.

Pastimes

South Africans play sports such as rugby, cricket, and squash. But because of apartheid, for many years people from South Africa were not allowed to take part in games with other countries, including the Olympics. Now, this has changed.

Today, blacks and whites play together in South Africa. And together, they are champions. South Africa sent a team to the Olympics for the first time in many years in 1992. In South Africa, many sports help blacks and whites work together as a team.

Xhosa boys play soccer near the water.

Holidays

South Africans celebrate a special holiday every December 16. In the past, many people honored those who died in a great battle between the Europeans and the Zulu. Today, this holiday reminds the people of South Africa to work together for peace. People in South Africa also celebrate on April 27. On this day in 1994, black and white South Africans voted together for the first time. This national holiday is called Freedom Day.

South Africa is a beautiful country with many things to see. The special mix of people, animals, plants, and food makes South Africa a very interesting place to live—and to visit! Maybe one day, you will see this special country for yourself.

December 16 is a day to celebrate South Africa's future.

Area: 471,010 square miles (1,219,912 square kilometers)—about two times the size of Texas

Population: About 44 million people

Capital Cities: Pretoria (administrative), Cape Town (legislative), and Bloemfontein (judicial)

Other Important Cities: Johannesburg, Soweto, Durban, and Port Elizabeth

Money: The rand. One rand is divided into 100 cents.

National Languages: There are 11 official languages: Afrikaans, English, and nine Bantu languages (Ndebele, Pedi, Sotho, Swazi, Tsonga, Tswana, Venda, Xhosa, and Zulu)

National Holiday: Freedom Day on April 27 (1994)

National Flag: Red, yellow, white, green, blue, and black. The way the colors are placed on the flag have a very special meaning. All of the colors join into a single stripe. The stripe reminds the people of South Africa to live together in peace.

Head of Government: The president of South Africa

Head of State: The president of South Africa

National Song: In 1996, *"Nkosi Sikelel' iAfrika"* ("God Bless Africa" in the Xhosa language) and "The Call of South Africa" were combined and shortened into the current national song. It includes words from five of South Africa's official languages— Sotho, Xhosa, Zulu, Afrikaans, and English.

> Lord, bless Africa
> May her spirit rise high up,
> Hear thou our prayers
> Lord bless us.
>
> Lord, bless Africa,
> Banish wars and strife,
> Lord, bless our nation,
> Of South Africa.
>
> Ringing out from our blue heavens,
> From our deep seas breaking round,
> Over everlasting mountains,
> Where the echoing crags resound,
>
> Sounds the call to come together,
> And united we shall stand,
> Let us live and strive for freedom,
> In South Africa our land.

Famous People:

Christiaan Barnard: heart surgeon

Stephen Biko: political activist

Johnny Clegg: musician

J. M. Coetzee: winner of the Nobel Prize for Literature in 2003

F. W. de Klerk: president of South Africa from 1989 to 1994 and cowinner of the Nobel Peace Prize in 1993

Nadine Gordimer: winner of the Nobel Prize for Literature in 1991

Miriam Makeba: musician

Nelson Mandela: president of South Africa from 1994 to 1999 and cowinner of the Nobel Peace Prize in 1993

Gary Player: golfer

Shaka: Zulu chief

Charlize Theron: actor

Desmond Tutu: winner of the Nobel Peace Prize in 1984

Desmond Tutu

South African Folktale:
"Words As Sweet As Honey from Sankhambi"

In the past, monkeys were not as thin and quick as they are today. A crafty creature named Sankhambi used to creep up behind them and yank their tails. In return, the monkey would throw seeds and twigs at Sankhambi. One day, Sankhambi tricked the monkeys to come with him to eat sweet honey in a mountain cave. When they reached the cave, Sankhambi shouted that the roof of the cave was falling in. He told the monkeys to stretch up their arms and hold up the roof while he ran to fetch some poles. He never returned—and that is how the bodies of the monkeys became tall and slender!

29

ENGLISH	AFRIKAANS	HOW TO SAY IT
hello	hallo	HAH-low
good-bye	tot siens	TAWT SEENZ
please	asseblief	AHS-suh-BLEEF
thank you	danke	DAHN-kee
one	een	EE-uhn
two	twee	TWEE
three	drie	DREE
South Africa	Suid-Afrika	SITE-AH-free-kuh

30

Glossary

Afrikaans (ah-free-KAANTZ) Afrikaans is a language that developed from the Dutch of the 1600s. It is one of several official languages of South Africa.

apartheid (uh-PAR-tite) Apartheid was a system that the old South African government used. Under apartheid, laws gave white people special rights over those who were not white.

Bantu (BAN-too) Bantu is a group of people from southern and central Africa. Bantu is also the family of languages these people speak.

continents (KON-tih-nents) Most of the land areas on Earth are divided up into huge sections called continents. South Africa is on the continent of Africa.

ethnic groups (ETH-nik GROOPS) Ethnic groups are groups of people who share a way of life, language, or race. There are many different ethnic groups in South Africa.

free elections (FREE ee-LEK-shuhnz) In free elections, the people vote for their leaders in a fair way. Free elections were held for the first time in South Africa in 1994.

mealie pap (MEE-lee PUP) Mealie pap is a favorite food in South Africa. It is a porridge made of corn and milk.

plateaus (pla-TOHZ) Plateaus are areas that are higher than the areas of land around them. South Africa's plateaus are surrounded by mountains.

Further Information

Read It

Hamilton, Janice. *South Africa in Pictures*. Minneapolis, MN: Lerner Publications, 2004.

Heale, Jay. *South Africa*. Milwaukee, WI: Gareth Stevens, 1998.

Kramer, Ann. *Mandela: The Rebel Who Led His Nation to Freedom*. Washington, DC: National Geographic, 2005.

Sisulu, Elinor, and Sharon Wilson (illustrator). *The Day Gogo Went to Vote*. Boston, MA: Little, Brown, 1996.

Look It Up

Visit our Web page for lots of links about South Africa:
http://www.childsworld.com/links

Note to Parents, Teachers, and Librarians: We routinely verify our Web links to make sure they are safe, active sites—so encourage your readers to check them out!

Index